MW00390726

impact discipleship

SPIRITUAL MATURITY WORKBOOK

OnePubishing Group
Los Angeles, California - Dallas, Texas

ISBN-10: 1719283214

OnePublishing Group
2945 Frankford Road
Dallas, Texas 75287

Crown Agency, cover art
Dr. Kwesi R. Kamau, Developer

First Edition
Printed in the United States of America

CONTENTS

INTRODUCTION
DISCIPLESHIP & DISCIPLEMAKING

There is a great need for the ministry of discipleship. Disciplemaking is the one thing Christ asked us to do as the mission of the Church. Yet, as LeRoy Eims suggests in the title of his book, The Lost Art of Disciple Making, disciplemaking is often the last thing the Church seeks to do. It is a "lost art" that many are eagerly seeking to recover.

Discipleship is related to but different from, evangelism. Evangelism is the process of establishing Christian communities where they were not formerly present. Discipleship is the work of making people faithful, mature followers of Jesus Christ. The two ideas work together to transform lives and to transform communities.

Discipleship is related to but different from, community service. A disciple is a servant of others and engaging in service opportunities is a great way to develop disciples. However, serving others is not all that it takes. People need more than just material things. We need spiritual support. We need the life-giving, life-transforming Word of God.

Discipleship is about loving people and leading them to a better life in Christ (*"loving people to life"*). It is about engaging, empowering, and equipping believers to fulfill the role that they were created to play faithfully. Discipleship creates leaders—not for positions, but for mission.

The IMPACT Discipleship Method involves 5 Series that progress from reaching the unchurched to training effective disciplemaking disciples. Series 1 involves witnessing to the unchurched and helping them see God's story from the Bible in their personal life story. Series 2 exposes people to the full gospel story through the stages of Creation, Corruption, Covenant, Christ, the Church, and the New Creation. Series 3 shares the six foundational principles of Christ from Hebrews 6:1-2: repentance, faith, baptism, spiritual authority, future resurrections, and eternal judgment. Series 4 and 5 group disciples into small training groups to learn the Spiritual Maturity Pathway and how to effectively disciple others. This Spiritual Maturity Workbook is material for Series 4.

discipleship

HOW TO USE THIS WORKBOOK

IMPACT DISCIPLESHIP METHOD

The Spiritual Maturity Workbook is a tool for Christian disciples who have a basic understanding of the Gospel and the foundational teachings of Christ outlined in Heb. 6:1-2.

This Workbook is designed to be a guide to aid new disciples and coaches in learning how to walk through the Spiritual Maturity Pathway. It contains

1) Meaningful examinations of relevant Bible passages
2) Powerful growth principles and examples
3) Helpful diagrams and illustrations
4) Engaging homework assignments

Each session will expose you to a new growth principle and will help you discern and experience the work of the Holy Spirit in your life.

Each Session Includes time to:

REFLECT

Each week the lesson starts with 20 minutes of discussion where the group can reflect on the ways the Holy Spirit has been moving in every person's life.

LEARN

After this opening, the group will take 40 minutes to study the prepared lesson which explains each new growth principle and presents a spiritual practice related to the lesson.

LOOK

At the close of each lesson, each person is prepared and challenged to look for ways the Holy Spirit is working in their lives to bring about spiritual maturity.

In addition, homework is assigned that involves reading through the Gospel of John, which contains a clear explanation of who Jesus is in his own words.

This Discipleship Method uses two approaches:

DISCIPLESHIP SMALL GROUPS

This small group takes a 1-on-3 approach, with a discipleship coach providing spiritual direction for three disciples. This tightly-knit group works through the lessons together and helps each other recognize the work of the Holy Spirit in one another's lives.

DSGs practice the power of Christian fellowship. The goal of each session is to train disciples to clearly identify and consistently follow the leading of the Holy Spirit as the Spirit develops in them the character of Christ.

SPIRITUAL MATURITY PATHWAY

This seven-week course outlines three stages and seven steps of spiritual maturity that leads a Christ-follower into becoming a fruitful disciple-making disciple of Jesus Christ. These stages and steps are listed as follows:

STAGE ONE – DEPENDENCE

Level 1. Seeing Things God's Way

Level 2. Putting Christ & Others First

Level 3. Personal Freedom from Past, Pain, and Pleasure

STAGE TWO – INDEPENDENCE

Level 4. Personal Clarity & Consistency

Level 5. Fellowship – Working Together with Wisdom

Level 6. Kingdom Prayer

STAGE THREE - FRUITION

Level 7. At-One-Ment

It's A Guide, Not A Manual

This resource is purposefully called a "workbook" rather than a "manual" or "lesson book." DSGs should only use this material as a guide for discussion and a general source for information about the process of spiritual growth. If God is bringing wisdom and understanding through discussion of the homework or people are experiencing a God-encounter in one area of the lesson, a coach should discern whether it is better to "stay right there" or to move to some of the other important principles in the lesson.

The DSG is purposefully Holy Spirit-driven and activity-centered. Therefore, it is much more important to find and emphasize a meaningful connection with the Spirit of God than it is to walk through the content of each chapter.

A Helpful Appendix

In the back of this DSG Workbook is a short appendix which includes an explanation of the biblical model for this process.

The Spiritual Maturity Pathway used in this process is built on principles found in the study of the Tabernacle of Moses. Much like the churches and Cathedrals of the Middle Ages, which taught the lessons of the Gospel through their architecture and stain glass windows, the pattern underlying the Tabernacle of Moses teaches essential lessons about spiritual life and maturity.

~

Some lessons in this Workbook will not be new to the mature disciple. You may find them, instead, to be a confirmation of your process of growth. What can be insightful for the mature disciple is to see how these lessons fit in an entire process of spiritual growth.

This Workbook is meant to help you see where you are spiritually, first. After you have learned to discern your own spiritual growth, you will be able to see where others might be on their journey. This insight is immensely helpful and useful in guiding others successfully along a spiritual growth path.

As we begin, let us pray the following prayer together.

Lord Jesus, may the wisdom and truth of your Word enlighten us and make us fruitful in developing disciple-making disciples and fulfilling the Great Commission in this generation. Amen.

THE ROADMAP

MESSAGE TO THE GROWING DISCIPLE

As a disciple of Jesus Christ, you are anointed to make an impact. Believe it or not, the whole world is waiting for you to become what you were meant to be. (Rom. 8:9)

You are meant to be an inspiration. God wants to fill your life with so much love and power that it overflows into the lives of others. This is key. Paul, the apostle, shared this principle in what can best be described as the most beautiful prayer for discipleship:

> *For this reason I kneel before the Father, from whom every family in heaven and on earth derives its name. I pray that out of his glorious riches he may strengthen you with power through his Spirit in your inner being, so that Christ may dwell in your hearts through faith. And I pray that you, being rooted and established in love, may have power, together with all the Lord's holy people, to grasp how wide and long and high and deep is the love of Christ, and to know this love that surpasses knowledge—that you may be filled to the measure of all the fullness of God.*—Ephesians 3:14-19

This prayer is for you.

A FULL LIFE

Your life is meant to be full and meaningful. (John 10:10) Nothing in this life or the life to come compares to being fully connected with God's love and purpose. God will transform this world through His crazy, hard-headed, life-transforming love, and He wants to start with you.

What does a full life look like? You will experience God more in your daily life and see everyday miracles and wonders. You will become more fruitful with a Christ-like character and in good works. And, you will never enjoy yourself so much, or feel so much that you belong. You will overflow with God's love and power, and this will impact <u>everyone</u> around you.

IT'S THE HOLY SPIRIT

You cannot experience this amazing fullness through your own efforts. The Bible says, "God works in you to will and to act in order to fulfill his good purpose." (Phil. 2:13) God knows where God wants to take you. Only the Spirit of God can develop the heart of Christ in you. He is the *true* disciplemaker.

Your job is to see God working in your life, and it is to follow Him. You must work through your personal transformation with "fear and trembling." (Phil. 2:12) The Holy Spirit knows how to cultivate fruitful Christians, and He has a process. Learn this process, and you will experience significant growth in your life.

WHAT TO EXPECT

This workbook is simply a tool to help you understand the spiritual growth process and to help you become more fruitful in your walk with Jesus Christ.

During the seven sessions of this Discipleship Small Group, you will learn how to follow the Spirit and to submit to God's work in your life more obediently. You will learn to see God's hand, hear God's voice, and feel God's presence better as God works to make you more like Jesus.

God does not need a mass of people to transform the world. One deeply rooted disciple who has learned how to be fruitful can multiply his/herself one hundred times over.

step one

SEEING THINGS GOD'S WAY

stage one: dependence

reflect

>> WELCOME EVERYONE TO THE FIRST SESSION.
>> LET EACH PERSON SHARE FROM THE FOLLOWING QUESTIONS:

When was the last time you sensed the Spirit of God leading you to do something important?

Has there been a time you felt like you missed God's leading for you to do something? What was it?

>> REVIEW GROUND RULES FOR GROUP SESSIONS.

Be prepared and ready to review assignments. The homework and exercises are designed to help you practice fellowshipping with the Holy Spirit and following His leading.

Be open. Everyone shares. Group members should find ways to affirm one another as they share. Also, no one should dominate the conversation.

Be timely. The group is scheduled to meet for 75 minutes. Everyone should be ready to both start and end on time.

learn

>>READ TOGETHER AND FILL IN THE BLANKS.
>>LEARN GROWTH THROUGH CRISIS, WISDOM, CHARACTER, & ENCOUNTER

The Dynamics of Spiritual Growth

Principle #1: Growth Comes through Crisis

[2]Consider it pure joy, my brothers and sisters, whenever you face trials of many kinds, [3]because you know that the testing of your faith produces perseverance. [4]Let perseverance finish its work so that you may be mature and complete, not lacking anything.—James 1:2-4

Pure Joy (v.2). Begins with an Anticipation of joyful expectation.

Many Kinds (v.2). Your Crisis______ or trial is a test.

Testing (vv.3-4). You grow when you pass the Test________; The test will involve a crisis of faith and a major adjustment in your life.

> *"Crisis is the bridge to growth and greater character."*

Principle #2: Ask and Wait for Wisdom to Grow

[5]If any of you lacks wisdom, you should ask God, who gives generously to all without finding fault, and it will be given to you. [6]But when you ask, you must believe and not doubt, because the one who doubts is like a wave of the sea, blown and tossed by the wind. [7]That person should not expect to receive anything from the Lord. [8]Such a person is double-minded and unstable in all they do.—James 1:5-8

Ask for Wisdom (v.5). When you are in a C____________, and you ask God for guidance, you will receive it. Be willing to seek help from others when you need it.

Wait for Wisdom (vv.6-7). You have to be P____________ and trust God to guide you. Do not rush to action.

 Answers: attitude, crisis, test, crisis, patient

> *Not only so, but we also glory in our sufferings, because we know that suffering produces perseverance; perseverance, character; and character, hope.*
> **—Romans 5:3-4**

5 Facts About the Spiritual Maturity Pathway

The following are general facts about growing spiritually.

1. There are Seven Steps and Three Stages in the Spiritual Maturity Pathway. You must go through each level in order.
2. As you begin to understand each level, the Holy Spirit will guide you through a test. When you pass the test, you gain experience and build up your character. When you don't pass, you get a re-test. (PS 38 God uses pain to cause us to turn around.)
3. For the first three levels, you will be in a stage of dependence. You need more motivation, advice, instruction, and support at this stage.
4. The second three levels, you should be more independent and self-directed. However, don't be fooled into thinking you have reached maturity. You still have a ways to go.
5. The seventh level is the third stage, where you are mature and consistently bearing all the fruit of the Spirit. (Corrie Ten Boom - unwavering faith in what she heard from God.)

How do you usually handle crisis?

Have you ever experienced God leading you through a crisis?

Have you ever had to take a "re-test" in life?

Character

Character is your ability to lead yourself in the right way. Spiritual maturity develops character at the same time it develops faith. These two sides of maturity—faith and character are needed to have fruitfulness and is abundant, and that lasts. While faith deepens your experience with God, character balances it. Faith allows you experience abundant blessings. Character empowers you to maintain the blessings. Character provides integrity, supports faithfulness and brings consistency to your walk with Christ.

> *Character cannot be developed in ease and quiet. Only through experience of trial and suffering can the soul be strengthened, ambition inspired, and success achieved.*
> *—Helen Keller*

Principle #3: Add Character to Your Faith

> *[5] For this very reason, make every effort to add to your faith goodness; and to goodness, knowledge; [6] and to knowledge, self-control; and to self-control, perseverance; and to perseverance, godliness; [7] and to godliness, mutual affection; and to mutual affection, love. [8] For if you possess these qualities in increasing measure, they will keep you from being ineffective and unproductive in your knowledge of our Lord Jesus Christ.—2 Peter 1:5-8*

Make Every Effort (v.5). Throughout your growth process, you must continually seek to A___________ faith to your character.

Quality Characteristics (vv.5-7). Disciples should apply the eight quality characteristics—faith, goodness, knowledge, self-control, perseverance, godliness, mutual affection, love—as a S_________ for living.

They Will Keep You (v.8). When you try to faithfully keep the standards for living, you will find they will keep you focused on powerfully E___________ God in your life.

 Answers: add, standard, experiencing

What is "Seeing Things God's Way?"

Principle #4: Encounter God

3 Jesus replied, "Very truly I tell you, no one can see the kingdom of God unless they are born again." 4 "How can someone be born when they are old?" Nicodemus asked. "Surely they cannot enter a second time into their mother's womb to be born!" 5 Jesus answered, "Very truly I tell you, no one can enter the kingdom of God unless they are born of water and the Spirit. 6 Flesh gives birth to flesh, but the Spirit gives birth to spirit.—John 3:1-5

Born Again (v.3). If you are going to "see things God's way" you have to have a "B__________ A__________" experience. This experience is likened to being "born-again" because it brings a feeling of new life as God awakens you to God's presence in your life.

See and Enter (vv. 3,5). You must S__________ the kingdom before you can enter it. You cannot begin a life of discipleship without seeing things God's way. This is the first step.

Encounter (v.6). *"Flesh, flesh; Spirit, spirit."* This play on words shows that a spiritual experience requires a real E__________ with God through the Holy Spirit.

"The person without the Spirit does not accept the things that come from the Spirit of God but considers them foolishness, and cannot understand them because they are discerned only through the Spirit. The person with the Spirit makes judgments about all things, but such a person is not subject to merely human judgments..."—1 Corinthians 2:14-20

"An experience with the Holy Spirit causes you to see things differently."

Answers: born, again, see, encounter

Seeing Means Understanding

Job 42:5-6 says, "My ears had heard of you, but now my eyes have seen you. Therefore, I despise myself and repent in dust and ashes." Below are four essential lessons about seeing.

1. Hearing and seeing have two different effects. Hearing brings faith and knowledge. (Rom. 10:17) Seeing brings understanding.
2. There is also a difference between knowledge and understanding. An excess of knowledge puffs up. (1 Cor. 8:1) Seeing things God's way always humbles.
3. Understand is "seeing under" what is "standing." It is the ability to see what is there beyond the surface.
4. Seeing things God's way gives us proper understanding. It is an ability that begins with being born-again and grows as we continue to experience God through the Bible.

SEEING = UNDERSTANDING

A good example of understanding is found in Psalm 103:7, where the Psalmist compares Moses, the man of God, and Israel. It says, "He [God] made known his ways to Moses, his deeds to the people of Israel."

Rick Warren, pastor of Saddleback Community Church and best-selling author, summarizes this statement:

> *"The people of Israel got to see what God did, but Moses got to understand why God did it."*

- I can trust You because I have seen You work in me + around me.
- I can't control what goes on but I can choose to trust Him

How We See Differently

Principle #5: Count God in

[5] Trust in the LORD with all your heart and lean not on your own understanding; [6] in all your ways submit to him, and he will make your paths straight.—Prov. 3:5,6

An act of will

Trust God (v.5). Choose to T__________ that God is active in your life and at work around you.

Lean Not (v.5). Do not depend solely on your sight and logic to work things out. There are often things going on that you do not see. Also, often your A__________ is different than God's agenda.

Submit (v.6). Acknowledge the reality of God in your life and submit to God's guidance and P__________.

"God is always at work in our lives. We simply have to take the time to notice."

We can too often be wrapped up in our own world and not take the time to notice God at work around us. When we take the time to see beyond the surface, it can powerfully transform our lives.

Steven Covey, author of *Seven Habits of Highly Effective People*, tells a compelling story about seeing things differently. He talks about being on a busy New York subway train one evening after a stressful day at work. The scene is quiet and peaceful until a man jumps on-board with his children. The children are very rambunctious and, frankly, irritating. What is more frustrating is that the man is doing nothing about it. Covey talks about how he uses what he felt was "unusual patience and restraint" and confronts the man.

"Sir, your children are really disturbing a lot of people. I wonder if you couldn't control them a little more?" The man, apparently emerging from a daze, looks around and says, "Oh, you are right. I am sorry. I was lost in thought. It's just ... we just left the hospital. My wife just died, and I don't know how to tell my kids."

Have you ever had an experience like this one?

Answers: trust, agenda, perspective

practice: GO TO CHURCH

The best way for people who are beginning their walk with Christ by learning how to see things God's way is to participate in a local church. In a local fellowship, you learn by example how to see God in everyday life, and you discover God's story.

The Church also offers a few unique things that help you see things God's way. Here are two important ones:

>> BAPTISM.

Baptism is an amazing experience where you celebrate your salvation by faith and are formally accepted into God's holy community. (Acts 2:38; Rom. 6:3-4)

In Baptism, you learn how to pattern your life on Christ. In baptism, you die with Christ and are buried. Then, you are raised with Christ with new life as a part of God's New Creation.

>> LORD'S SUPPER.

In the Lord's Supper, you fully remind yourself how Jesus gave his body and blood on a cross for the forgiveness of your sins. (Matt. 26:26-28)

In the Lord's Supper, God mysteriously encounters you in the bread and cup, and this encounter strengthens your faith and understanding.

REVIEW THE **PRACTICE** ABOVE.REMIND EVERYONE TO **LOOK** FOR THE HOLY SPIRIT IN THEIR DAILY LIVES THROUGHOUT THE WEEK AND TO COMPLETE THE HOMEWORK EXERCISES.

look

>>LOOK FOR THE DECISION-MAKING MOMENTS THROUGHOUT THIS WEEK.

>>REFLECT EACH NIGHT ON HOW WELL YOU NOTICED GOD IN THOSE MOMENTS.

Write down a snapshot of one experience you have this week with seeing things God's way.

WEEKDAY HOMEWORK

Complete assignment for each day:

day one >> **READ John 1-3 completely. Ask the 5 "W" and the 5 Senses questions.**

who, what, when, where, why?

what can you see, hear, taste, touch, and/or smell?

day two >> *How does John 1:1-18 relate to Genesis 1 and 2? Do you see any patterns?*

day three>> *Jesus said that his "hour had not yet come." What does this say about how God works in our lives?*

day four>> *What do you think John 3:3-8 teaches about the experience of the Holy Spirit? Why is this important to seeing things God's way?*

day five>> *How many different ways is Jesus described, or does he describe himself, in John's first three chapters?*

REVIEW OF CHAPTER

This chapter covered the following:

- Understanding how spiritual growth happens

- Outlining the Spiritual Maturity Pathway

- What it means to see things God's way

- How to practice seeing differently

STAGE ONE – DEPENDENCE

Level 1. Seeing Things God's Way

Do you see things God's way? Do you submit to it?

Level 2. Putting Christ & Others First

Do Christ and others take priority in your thinking?

Level 3. Personal Freedom from Past, Pain, and Pleasure

Have you faced up to your issues ("your stuff") and put the past in the past?

STAGE TWO – INDEPENDENCE

Level 4. Personal Clarity & Consistency

Are you independently consistent in the Word and Fellowship w/ God? Do you manage your life (time) and resources (money) based on Christ's mission?

Level 5. Working Together with Wisdom

Are you intellectually and emotionally mature enough to do championship teamwork?

Level 6. Kingdom Prayer

Does purposeful prayer fully undergird your life?

STAGE THREE - FRUITION

Level 7. At-ONE-Ment

You are full of the grace of the Holy Spirit and fully available for Christ to live and work through you.

step two

PUTTING CHRIST & OTHERS FIRST

stage one: dependence

reflect

>> WELCOME EVERYONE TO THE SESSION.
>> LET EACH PERSON SHARE FROM THE FOLLOWING QUESTION:

What did the Holy Spirit say or do in your life this past week that helped you practice seeing things God's way?

>> REVIEW HOMEWORK.

How does John 1:1-18 relate to Genesis 1 and 2? Do you see any patterns?

Why did Jesus say that his "hour had not yet come"? What does this say about how God works in our lives?

What do you think John 3:3-8 teaches about the experience of the Holy Spirit? Why is this important to see things God's way?

How many different ways is Jesus described or does he describe himself in John's first three chapters?

learn

>>READ TOGETHER AND FILL IN THE BLANKS.

>>LEARN TO LEAD, SACRIFICE, & IDENTIFY WITH OTHERS WITH A SINCERE HEART

Follow the Example of Christ

Principle #1: Lead through serving

25 Jesus called them together and said, "You know that the rulers of the Gentiles lord it over them, and their high officials exercise authority over them. 26 Not so with you. Instead, whoever wants to become great among you must be your servant, 27 and whoever wants to be first must be your slave—28 just as the Son of Man did not come to be served, but to serve, and to give his life as a ransom for many."—Matthew 20:25-28

Worldly Leadership (v.25). Jesus makes a sharp distinction between L__________ as we generally see it in the world and leadership from his perspective. There is a difference.

Greatness (v.26). Jesus does not measure G__________ by power, but by how we add value to others.

Christ's Example (v.28). Jesus exemplified true leadership and demonstrated true greatness by being a S__________ to others.

"Jesus exercised his power by adding value to others, rather than simply building up himself."

This is my commandment, that you love one another as I have loved you.

—John 15:12

 Answers: leadership, greatness, servant

"The real value of life is the value you add to others."

Principle #2: True service in self-sacrificial

[1]Therefore, I urge you, brothers and sisters, in view of God's mercy, to offer your bodies as a living sacrifice, holy and pleasing to God—this is your true and proper worship. [2]Do not conform to the pattern of this world, but be transformed by the renewing of your mind. Then you will be able to test and approve what God's will is—his good, pleasing and perfect will.—Romans 12:1-2

Mercy (v.1). God's M__________ brings out a desire to show mercy. It is the inspiration for us to put others first.

Blessed are the merciful, for they will be shown mercy.—Matthew 5:7

Be a Giver (v.1). Being an "living S__________" involves living sacrificially. It means you give of yourself, regarding other's needs before your own.

Be devoted to one another in love. Honor one another above yourselves.—Romans 12:10

Renewed Mind (v.2). A living sacrifice depends on a change of mind. You have to see things God's way to put Christ and others first.

... be made new in the attitude of your minds.—Ephesians 4:23

JOY (v.2). A life of sacrifice is the secret to J__________, in which you show God's "good, pleasing, and perfect will." J-O-Y means Jesus first, Others second, Yourself last.

Christ made his life about serving others. Putting Christ and others first requires that we develop his character of self-sacrifice, humility, and a sincere love for others.

How do we usually measure success?

How does Christ's definition of success compare?

Answers: mercy, sacrifice, joy

How to Live for Others

Principle #4: Identify with others.

[13] Share with the Lord's people who are in need. Practice hospitality. [14] Bless those who persecute you; bless and do not curse. [15] Rejoice with those who rejoice; mourn with those who mourn. [16] Live in harmony with one another. Do not be proud, but be willing to associate with people of low position. Do not be conceited.—Romans 12:13-16

Hospitality (v.13). H__________ is one of the most important virtues in the Bible.

Attentiveness (vv.14-16). A life of sacrifice is being faithfully A__________ to others, being present with others in good times and bad. It invites others into your life as well.

Principle #3: Service from a sincere heart.

[9] Love must be sincere. Hate what is evil; cling to what is good. [10] Be devoted to one another in love. Honor one another above yourselves. —Romans 12:9-10

Sincerity (v.9). Sincerity is key. Love F__________ on others for others' sake.

Devotion (v.10). Self-sacrifice is an act of D__________ to Christ and to others. It is always honoring others before yourself.

"A new command I give you: Love one another. As I have loved you, so you must love one another. By this everyone will know that you are my disciples, if you love one another."—John 13:34-35

How can you show sincerity, devotion, hospitality, or attentiveness to others in your life?

 Answers: Hospitality, attentive, focused, devotion

For by the grace given me I say to every one of you: Do not think of yourself more highly than you ought, but rather think of yourself with sober judgment, in accordance with the faith God has distributed to each of you.
—Romans 12:3

"Pride makes us artificial. Humility makes us real." – Thomas Merton

3 Facts about Humility

The following are general facts about humility.

1. Humility is not putting yourself D__________. It is lifting God up.
2. Humility is the S__________ to be honest about our weaknesses.
3. Humility calls us to do G__________ things. When God gives you a great gift, humility calls you to use it with excellence.

How is this similar or different from how you have seen humility?

Answers: down, strength, greater

Depending on the Holy Spirit

Your spiritual growth depends on the Holy Spirit. As we have seen, He works through the situations of your life to help you grow. He also works in you to bring about growth. The Spirit brings about faith as you dynamically experience Him. Here are four key ways we experience the Holy Spirit.

He Awakens You

The Spirit's first role is to awaken you to God's activity in your life, leading your conversion ultimately to Christ. Jesus talked about this experience with the Holy Spirit like this:

> *When he comes, he will prove the world to be in the wrong about sin and righteousness and judgment: about sin, because people do not believe in me; about righteousness, because I am going to the Father, where you can see me no longer; and about judgment, because the prince of this world now stands condemned.*—John 16:7-11

When the Holy Spirit awakens you, He leads you to have a "born-again experience" where the Holy Spirit indwells you.

He Lives In (Indwells) You

Jesus told his disciples that the Holy Spirit would not only be with us to awaken us, but He would also come and live in us:

> *And I will ask the Father, and he will give you another advocate to help you and be with you forever—the Spirit of truth. The world cannot accept him, because it neither sees him nor knows him. But you know him, for he lives with you and will be in you. I will not leave you as orphans; I will come to you.—John 14:16-17*

In the Old Testament, back with Moses and Israel in the Wilderness, the Holy Tabernacle was dedicated, and God came to rest in it. (See Exodus 40:34-38) Again, when Solomon built the Temple in Jerusalem hundreds of years later, he dedicated it, and the glory of God came and rested there. (See 2 Chronides 7:1-3)

When you dedicate yourself to God, in the same way, the Holy Spirit comes to rest *in you.* You literally become a living, breathing temple!

He Fills You with Power

After the Holy Spirit comes to rest in you, He also empowers you. In the Bible, people were "filled with the Holy Spirit" to do great works. The Spirit empowers us to live faithfully as disciples of Christ, and He also gives us divine power to witness to the love of God in the world through answered prayer, gifts of healing, and other miraculous works.

Do not get drunk on wine, which leads to debauchery. Instead, be [continually] filled with the Spirit.—Ephesians 5:18

When the Spirit fills you, there is a stronger sense of connection with God that brings about things like boldness, peace, and a strong sense of direction.

You can be filled with the Holy Spirit through daily prayer, confession of God's Word, and submission to the Spirit's leading in particular moments. The filling of the Spirit is like drinking water. You have to do it day after day. The Bible says:

"You need to grow in both faith and character."

He Gives You the Fullness of God

While being "FILLED with the Spirit" represents God's empowerment, being "FULL of the Spirit" is a description of a person's maturity. For instance, Luke uses the word to describe suitable leaders in the church:

Brothers and sisters, choose seven men from among you who are known to be full of the Spirit and wisdom. We will turn this responsibility over to them.
—Acts 6:3

You are full of the Spirit when you are mature in faith and character. Remember, your faith relates to your experience with God. It is your trusting response to God's Word and God's activity in your life. Character, once again, is defined as your capacity to lead yourself according to good principles. It is measured in your ability to choose wisely and your consistently doing what is right.

practice: FASTING

Fasting is denying yourself basic nourishment through food and, sometimes, water. It is an act of self-denial for the sake of justice for others.

See Isaiah 58:3-10

The act of fasting accomplishes three major things:

>> BROKENNESS

Break the power of self-centeredness and sinful habits and desires by fasting and serving the needs of others. (Esth. 4:16)

>> MOURNING

Engage your heart in mourning injustice both interpersonally and systemically. (Ps. 35:13-14)

>> FOCUS.

Focus your mind, soul, and body in prayer to God. (Joel 2:12)

From the earliest times, Christians would fast until after midday on Wednesdays and Fridays. ***Practice fasting this week on one of these days. Fast and pray "Father, not my will, but Your will be done."***

REVIEW THE PRACTICE ON THE NEXT PAGE. REMIND EVERYONE TO **LOOK** FOR THE HOLY SPIRIT IN THEIR DAILY LIVES THROUGHOUT THE WEEK AND TO COMPLETE THE HOMEWORK EXERCISES.

look

>>LOOK FOR THE DECISION-MAKING MOMENTS THROUGHOUT THIS WEEK.
>>REFLECT EACH NIGHT ON HOW WELL YOU NOTICED GOD IN THOSE MOMENTS.

Write down a snapshot of one experience you have this week putting Christ and others first.

WEEKDAY HOMEWORK

Complete assignment for each day:

day one >> **READ John 4-7 completely. Ask the 5 "W" and the 5 Senses questions.**

who, what, when, where, why?

what can you see, hear, taste, touch, and/or smell?

day two >> *Read John 7:37-44. How do these verses relate to John 4?*

day three>> *How does Jesus show humility in John 6:16-30?*

day four>> *In what ways do you think we can apply Jesus' words, "Do not work for food that spoils, but for food that endures to eternal life?"*

day five>> *In Chapter 7, the people are amazed by Jesus'' words and his miracles. Yet, they still have trouble believing in him? In what ways is this true of Christians today?*

REVIEW OF CHAPTER

This chapter covered the following:

- How to follow Christ's example through service and self-sacrifice
- The power of living for others
- What real humility is
- The role of the Holy Spirit in our spiritual life and growth

STAGE ONE – DEPENDENCE

Level 1. Seeing Things God's Way

Do you see things God's way? Do you submit to it?

Level 2. Putting Christ & Others First

Do Christ and others take priority in your thinking?

Level 3. Personal Freedom from Past, Pain, and Pleasure

Have you faced up to your issues ("your stuff") and put the past in the past?

STAGE TWO – INDEPENDENCE

Level 4. Personal Clarity & Consistency

Are you independently consistent in the Word and Fellowship w/ God? Do you manage your life (time) and resources (money) based on Christ's mission?

Level 5. Working Together with Wisdom

Are you intellectually and emotionally mature enough to do championship teamwork?

Level 6. Kingdom Prayer

Does purposeful prayer fully undergird your life?

STAGE THREE - FRUITION

Level 7. At-ONE-Ment

You are full of the grace of the Holy Spirit and fully available for Christ to live and work through you.

step three

PERSONAL FREEDOM

stage one: dependence

reflect

>> WELCOME EVERYONE TO THE SESSION.
>> LET EACH PERSON SHARE FROM THE FOLLOWING QUESTION:

What did the Holy Spirit say or do in your life this past week that helped you put Christ and others first?

>> REVIEW HOMEWORK.

How does John 7:37-44 relate to what you read in John 4? Did you see how it dealt with the Holy Spirit?

Did you see how Jesus demonstrated humility in John 5:16-30?

In what ways do you think you can build your personal holiness? What spiritual practices can you use to build your faith in Christ?

Describe how people have trouble putting their trust in Jesus, even after he has shown them his love and power.

learn

>>READ TOGETHER AND FILL IN THE BLANKS.
>>LEARN TRUE FREEDOM THROUGH DISCIPLESHIP, CHRIST-LIKENESS, & SPIRITUAL RENEWAL

WHAT IS MEANT BY PERSONAL FREEDOM?

Personal freedom is our spiritual victory over past hang-ups, present pain, and the bondage of temptation.

Principle #1: Freedom comes through being a true disciple

31 To the Jews who had believed him, Jesus said, "If you hold to my teaching, you are really my disciples. 32 Then you will know the truth, and the truth will set you free." – John 8:31-32

Be a Disciple (v.31). The key to personal freedom is actively being a D__________. It is not enough to be a member of a church or claim to know God. A true disciple learns and lives out Jesus' teaching.

Know the Truth (v32). The phrase "know the truth" is more than simply knowing F__________ about God. In the Bible, you know God when you have in-depth experience with Him.

Freedom (v.32). When you experience the truth by following the teachings and example of Christ, you experience freedom from your P__________, your P__________, and your sinful passion.

> You have been set free from sin and have become slaves to righteousness.
> ***—Romans 8:16***

 Answers: disciple, facts, pain, past

WHAT DOES IT MEAN TO BE A DISCIPLE?

A disciple is a student, a servant, and a follower of Jesus Christ.

There are three ways to see what it means to be a disciple.

1. **Student.** A disciple is C___________ to learning the Word of God.

   "Do your best to present yourself to God as one approved, a worker who does not need to be ashamed and who correctly handles the word of truth."—2 Timothy 2:15

2. **Servant.** Disciples are servants to the cause of Christ by
   - ⇒ W__________ him (Matt. 28:16)
   - ⇒ Loving others (John 13:35)
   - ⇒ M__________ other disciples of Jesus Christ (John 15:16)

3. **Follower.** A disciple follows Jesus by
   - ⇒ W__________ by the power of the Spirit (Gal. 5:16)
   - ⇒ Living by Christ's example (Eph. 5:1-2)

To which characteristic of being a disciple do you most relate?

Answers: committed, Worshipping, Making, Walking

The Path to Personal Freedom

Principle #2: Freedom comes through being like Christ

[20]That, however, is not the way of life you learned [21]when you heard about Christ and were taught in him in accordance with the truth that is in Jesus. – Ephesians 4:20-21

A Way of Life (v.20). Here Paul encourages believers to walk W__________ of the call of Christ to be his disciples. In modern terms, we should not simply be M__________ of the Church, but disciples of Christ.

"As a prisoner for the Lord, then, I urge you to live a life worthy of the calling you have received."—Ephesians 4:1

Learning Christ (v.21). Discipleship is about becoming like Christ. Originally, we were made in the I__________ and L__________of God. (cf. Gen. 1:26; 4:1) In Christ, God restores His image in us. We are forgiven, and God restores us to our original design and purpose. Our role after this is to learn how to live like Christ lived, embracing his H__________ and C__________.

A Lifestyle of Freedom

Personal freedom is a lifestyle. You can only live this lifestyle successfully when you keep the example of Christ before you through worship, reading the Bible, consistent prayer, and staying in fellowship with other disciples.

For you were called to freedom, brothers. Only do not use your freedom as an opportunity for the flesh, but through love serve one another.—Galatians 5:1

When you are baptized, you commit to this lifestyle. In a real way, in baptism, you die to your old life and are buried—just like Jesus died for our sins and was buried. Then, you are raised to new life, like Jesus was raised from the dead.

In your new life in Christ, you see things God's way and practice putting Christ and others first. These preceding steps of spiritual growth prepare you to experience true personal freedom.

Are you prepared to truly experience your personal freedom?

 Answers: worthy, members, image, likeness, heart, character

Principle #3: Personal freedom involves a process of renewal

[22]You were taught, with regard to your former way of life, to put off your old self, which is being corrupted by its deceitful desires; [23]to be made new in the attitude of your minds; [24]and to put on the new self, created to be like God in true righteousness and holiness.—Ephesians 4:22-24

The Way to Personal Freedom

1) Put off the old self
2) Be renewed in attitude
3) Put on new self

Put Off Old Self (v.22). Putting off the old self is like taking off old dirty C__________. The "old clothes" in your life are faded, ragged, and smelly. What do the "old clothes" represent? They are faded D__________, ragged E__________, and "stinking thinking." We put them off by confessing them and rejecting them.

Renewed Attitude (v.23). The second step toward personal freedom is to be renewed in your attitude. We change from having an attitude of D__________, D__________, or bondage to our sinful desires, to an attitude of victory and hope. We learn to identify with our future in Christ, rather than our past in sin.

Put on Christ (v.24). The third step toward personal freedom is to "put on Christ." This picture drives you to take on a new self-image patterned on Jesus Christ and that you continue to develop the C__________ of Christ in your life.

Answers: clothes, dreams, emotions, despair, defeat, character

THE PROCESS OF RENEWAL

Washing Away Sin and its Effects

Being spiritually renewed is like taking a good, long bath. Actually, one bath will not do. It requires many washings to fully clean the heart from the deep-seated stains of the old life. There are several ways we wash our hearts:

Washing Guilt and Shame. We wash away the shame from failures by applying God's F__________ in Christ. We embrace with our heart the renewed image of God provided by Jesus Christ.

"How much more, then, will the blood of Christ, who through the eternal Spirit offered himself unblemished to God, cleanse our consciences from acts that lead to death, so that we may serve the living God!"—Hebrews 9:14

"If we confess our sins, he is faithful and just and will forgive us our sins and purify us from all unrighteousness."—1 John 1:9

Washing Woundedness. With natural wounds, we need to wash and cleanse them from infection. The same is true for spiritual and emotional wounds. The answer to our woundedness is true W__________ and prayer. The presence of God we experience in worship cleanses our infected hearts.

"He heals the brokenhearted and binds up their wounds."—Psalm 147:3

Washing Wicked Thoughts. Some thoughts and desires are persistent. However, we don't have to struggle with them forever. (The next few words are very important!) We can receive a clean heart as a M__________ from God.

"Create in me a [clean] heart, O God, and renew a steadfast spirit within me."—Psalm 50:10

> Blessed is the one whose transgressions are forgiven, whose sins are covered.
> ***—Psalm 32:1***

 Answers: forgiveness, worship, miracle

To have personal freedom, you have to give up your old way of life—your old way of thinking and your old way of feeling. ***Stop seeing yourself as a sinner*** *and see yourself as a* ***child of a holy God****. In Christ, you are redeemed, forgiven, and clean because of his sacrifice.*

MOVING PAST DEPENDENCE

When we begin our journey to spiritual maturity, we start as babes in Christ. We are dependent on others to feed us, nurture us, and protect us. This support is the role the person discipling you, as well as other mature Christ-followers in your life. You cannot mature adequately by yourself or with just "you and God."

As you learn to "see things God's way," "put Christ and others first," and attain "personal freedom from pain, past, and sinful passions," you naturally develop the skills to stand and walk with Christ without aid. You still need others! However, you gain enough independence to start feeding yourself. You become more self-motivated and self-directed. You are halfway through ... so, keep growing!

practice: CONFESSION

Confession is the practice of admitting you have sinned or declaring God's Gospel and His will for your life.

See James 5:16 & 2 Corinthians 9:13

There are three types of confession :

>> CONFESS SINS

Break the power of guilt and shame by confessing every wicked thought, word, or deed privately to God. God will forgive, cleanse, and renew. (1 John 1:8)

>> CONFESS FAULTS

Powerfully encounter God by sharing with other Christians your brokenness, faults, and failures. They will pray, and you will be healed. (Jas. 5:16)

>> CONFESS THE GOSPEL

Declare God's forgiveness and healing through the powerful work of Jesus Christ. (1 Pet. 2:24)

REVIEW THE PRACTICE ON THE NEXT PAGE. REMIND EVERYONE TO **LOOK** FOR THE HOLY SPIRIT IN THEIR DAILY LIVES THROUGHOUT THE WEEK AND TO COMPLETE THE HOMEWORK EXERCISES.

look

>>LOOK FOR THE DECISION-MAKING MOMENTS THROUGHOUT THIS WEEK.
>>REFLECT EACH NIGHT ON HOW WELL YOU NOTICED GOD IN THOSE MOMENTS.

Write down a snapshot of one experience you have this week with personal freedom.

WEEKDAY HOMEWORK

Complete assignment for each day:

day one >> **READ John 8-11 completely. Ask the 5 "W" and the 5 Senses questions.**

who, what, when, where, why?

what can you see, hear, taste, touch, and/or smell?

day two >> *In what ways does Jesus deal with sin in John 8:1-11?*

day three>> *Jesus talks about freedom in John 8:31-36. How do you picture the freedom that he gives?*

day four>> *How does Jesus cause the blind to see and those who see to become blind?*

day five>> *In what ways is Jesus the Good Shepherd? How is he a shepherd and how is he good?*

REVIEW OF CHAPTER

This chapter covered the following:

- We can have freedom from our past, our pain, and our personal temptations

- Our path to freedom involves being like Christ and allowing Christ to renew us

- We must see things God's way and put Christ and others first before we can experience true freedom

- Renewal involves being washed from sin, woundedness, and wicked thoughts

STAGE ONE – DEPENDENCE

Level 1. Seeing Things God's Way

Do you see things God's way? Do you submit to it?

Level 2. Putting Christ & Others First

Do Christ and others take priority in your thinking?

Level 3. Personal Freedom from Past, Pain, and Pleasure

Have you faced up to your issues ("your stuff") and put the past in the past?

STAGE TWO – INDEPENDENCE

Level 4. Personal Clarity & Consistency

Are you independently consistent in the Word and Fellowship w/ God? Do you manage your life (time) and resources (money) based on Christ's mission?

Level 5. Working Together with Wisdom

Are you intellectually and emotionally mature enough to do championship teamwork?

Level 6. Kingdom Prayer

Does purposeful prayer fully undergird your life?

STAGE THREE - FRUITION

Level 7. At-ONE-Ment

You are full of the grace of the Holy Spirit and fully available for Christ to live and work through you.

step four

PERSONAL CLARITY & CONSISTENCY

stage two: independence

reflect

>> WELCOME EVERYONE TO THE SESSION.
>> LET EACH PERSON SHARE FROM THE FOLLOWING QUESTION:

What did the Holy Spirit say or do in your life this past week that helped you experience personal freedom?

>> REVIEW HOMEWORK.

What are the ways in which Jesus deals with sin in John 8:1-11?

How does the truth make you free?

How does John 9:35-41 speak to issues of personal freedom?

How does Jesus guide us daily to personal freedom?

learn

>>READ TOGETHER AND FILL IN THE BLANKS.
>>LEARN SPIRITUAL DISCERNMENT, DISCIPLINE,

In the first three steps toward spiritual maturity, God clears the ground and prepares your heart and mind for the next stage. The next step is to lay a solid foundation for a life-long process of growing.

MOVE TOWARD MATURITY: FOUNDATIONS

There are six elementary teachings that the early church leaders used to lay a foundation for spiritual growth.

Hebrews 6:1-2 offers six foundational principles for maturity in Christ. These teachings ground you in the truth and motivate you to grow.

1 Therefore let us move beyond the elementary teachings about Christ and be taken forward to maturity, not laying again the foundation of repentance from acts that lead to death, and of faith in God, 2 instruction about cleansing rites, the laying on of hands, the resurrection of the dead, and eternal judgment.
—Hebrews 6:1-2

THE SIX FOUNDATION STONES

These principles are covered in Series 3 of the IMPACT Discipleship Method. Spiritual maturity is built on this foundation and a firm grasp of these Biblical teachings.

1. Repentance. (lit. "to turn around") We must turn away from "D__________ works" which deny God's Presence and power in our lives. Repentance is not just a moment. It is a process.

2. Faith. (lit. "trust; " also, belief, depend, guarantee, assurance, reliable) Our faith is <u>in</u> God. It is not a power. It is C__________ based on who God is to do what it is you need to do. It is also openness and obedience to God's will and God's way.

3. **Baptisms.** (lit. "washings") This initiation rite was often used as a symbol of W__________ away the old dirty life with its old relationships, and embracing a new one with a new "family." It stands as a sacrament of R__________ and I__________. (Cf. Rom. 6:1-14; 10:9)

4. **Laying Hands.** This was a rite of A__________. A leader would lay hands to invest blessing, authority, or power on another. (Cf. 2 Tim. 1:6)

5. Resurrection. In the future, Jesus will return in his resurrected body, and God will raise everyone who ever lived back to life, both good and bad. (1 Cor. 15:35-58)

6. Eternal Judgment. When Jesus returns he will judge everyone according to the fruit of our faith and God will R__________ according to whether we lived to God's glory or rejected the truth and followed evil. (Rom. 2:6-8; Rev. 20:11-15)

What do these six elementary teachings mean to you?

Which one of these foundational lessons catches your attention the most?

Answers: dead, conviction, washing, repentance, inclusion, authority, reward

THE SPIRIT-CONTROLLED LIFE

When we reach the growth-stage of independence, we see more and more the evidence of a life G__________ by the Spirit of God—a "Spirit-controlled" life.

REDEEMING YOUR STRENGTHS

We all have our own personal traits. These traits are strengths that God gave us. Yet, our natural S__________ takes our strengths and uses them against us. For instance, some of us are thoughtful, but we can be intense. Others are gentle and shy, but we can be too reclusive. We can be passionate, but let our anger get the best of us. Some people are care-free, but also careless and unreliable.

When the Spirit controls our personality, God smooths over our rough edges and redeems our strengths. We can truly be ourselves and use our strengths to B__________ others and S__________ the world. In this way, we are made to be like Jesus while at the same time living in our God-given uniqueness.

THE FRUIT OF THE SPIRIT'S WORK

The work of the Holy Spirit produces Christ-like character. Without the Holy Spirit working in you, you cannot truly be a Christian. In the beginning of the Christian journey, it is difficult to see the fruit of the Spirit's work. You will still have old sinful habits and personal rough-edges. Yet, as you grow, your Christ-likeness will be more evident.

> *The mind governed by the flesh is death, but the mind governed by the Spirit is life and peace.*—**Romans 8:6**

 Answers: guided, sinfulness, build, serve

EXERCISING PERSONAL CLARITY

Principle #1: Holy Spirit discernment provides personal clarity

But you have an anointing from the Holy One, and you know the truth. —1 John 2:20

Anointing. Christians are A__________ with the Holy Spirit. Jesus promised the Holy Spirit would lead us into all truth.

Now it is God who makes both us and you stand firm in Christ. He anointed us, set his seal of ownership on us, and put his Spirit in our hearts as a deposit, guaranteeing what is to come.—1 Cor. 1:21-22

But when he, the Spirit of truth, comes, he will guide you into all the truth. He will not speak on his own; he will speak only what he hears, and he will tell you what is yet to come.—John 16:13

Know Truth. John tells us that the Holy Spirit gives God's people a basic D__________ so that we can instinctively I__________ the truth. The more we experience God, free from our pain, our past, and our sinful passions, the greater our ability to see the truth.

When you see things God's way, put Christ and others first, and you are increasingly free from spiritual and emotional bondage, the cloud is lifted from your mind. You can pray better and receive direction from God's Word more clearly.

Answers: anointed, discernment, identify

GOD'S WORD TO *YOU*

One great benefit from this basic discernment is that we will understand God's Word better. It will become clearer and clearer, and we will understand how to apply God's Word more and more. The Bible instructs us to seek clarity from God's word.

> *"Do your best to present yourself to God as one approved, a worker who does not need to be ashamed and who correctly handles the word of truth."*—2 Timothy 2:15-16

We correctly handle God's Word through studying it properly. Here is a simple guide to Bible Study called the A-C-T-S Bible Study Method.

THE ACTS METHOD

A	Associate Let the Bible interpret itself. Use the reference column in your Bible and compare what the verse or passage says with other similar verses.
C	Context Look at the whole picture. Read the verses before and after to understand the flow. Figure out whether the verse is being descriptive – simply telling what happened – or proscriptive – telling us to do something.
T	Tools Use a Bible dictionary to understand Biblical terms and measurements. A concordance is used to look up every word of a verse used in the Bible. A good commentary will give you useful historical and cultural information.
S	Spirit-Led Always let the Spirit guide you. The Holy Spirit will show you what to study and will show you the practical application of what you are studying.

PRACTICING CONSISTENCY

Principle #2: Practice and Faith lead to personal consistency

For though I am absent from you in body, I am present with you in spirit and delight to see how disciplined you are and how firm your faith in Christ is.
—Colossians 2:5

Paul expresses in this verse his joy that the Colossians have grown to a point where they have consistency and clarity, without Paul having to be there. He describes this independence using the words D__________ and F__________.

Discipline. Consistency is built on disciplined practice. When we can pray and experience A__________, or read the Bible and gain understanding or guidance, we get motivated to prioritize these things. We discipline ourselves to do what is most meaningful to us.

Faith. Paul mentions faith as well. Sometimes discipline is not enough. Many things can arise to knock you off course. We need firmness of faith to ward off the D__________ and disappointments that work against our discipline. We must sometimes exercise our faith that God will speak or act even when it does not feel like God will.

Spiritual consistency begins with time spent with God in prayer and devotion to God's Word. It grows through sharing in the Lord's Supper, fellowship with others, giving and acts of service, fasting from food, and healthy living.

Answers: discipline, faith, answers, distractions

practice: OPEN BIBLE

Personal devotion to God's Word is the cornerstone to developing personal clarity and consistency. Below is a beginners method to develop discipline and faith.

THE FIFTEEN MINUTE DEVOTION

:00 - :05	For the first five minutes, thank God for every blessing, large or small. Consider God's grace from the former day, week, month, or year. Thank God verbally.
:05 - :10	Read one Psalm or a Chapter in Proverbs. One can read from both books when having a morning and evening devotion. Find one or two verses that grab your heart or attention.
:10 - :15	Read over that one (or two) verse several times. Ask God to show you why the verse is relevant to your day.

If you are just starting out with a discipline of praying, spend a week practicing fifteen minutes of devotion. You may run out of time but stick to the fifteen minutes. The more you do it, you will likely start running out of time. Do not go over. You can find space later in the day to finish.

If you are more experienced in having personal devotions, try 30 minutes or an hour a day for the week. Stick to the schedule. Start on time and end on time. You can adjust your time length for the next week when you need to do so.

REVIEW THE PRACTICE ON THE NEXT PAGE. REMIND EVERYONE TO **LOOK** FOR THE HOLY SPIRIT IN THEIR DAILY LIVES THROUGHOUT THE WEEK AND TO COMPLETE THE HOMEWORK EXERCISES.

look

>>LOOK FOR THE DECISION-MAKING MOMENTS THROUGHOUT THIS WEEK.
>>REFLECT EACH NIGHT ON HOW WELL YOU NOTICED GOD IN THOSE MOMENTS.

Write down a snapshot of one experience you have this week with clarity and consistency.

WEEKDAY HOMEWORK

Complete assignment for each day:

day one >> READ John 12-14 completely. Ask the 5 "W" and the 5 Senses questions.

who, what, when, where, why?

what can you see, hear, taste, touch, and/or smell?

day two >> *How do we grow in understanding according to John 12:16?*

day three>> *Jesus predicted Peter would fail him at a very critical moment. How do you react when you fail God in important things? How should you react, with John 13:38 in mind?*

day four>> *Jesus is "the way, the truth, and the life." How can the life of Jesus help you understand God's Word better?*

day five>> *Based on John 14:23-26, how do you develop clarity and consistency in your walk with Christ?*

REVIEW OF CHAPTER

This chapter covered the following:

- The six foundational principles for spiritual maturity
- How the Spirit-controlled life enhances our lives
- How to study God's Word effectively
- How to receive personal clarity through the Holy Spirit
- Developing personal consistency through practice and faith

STAGE ONE – DEPENDENCE

Level 1. Seeing Things God's Way

Do you see things God's way? Do you submit to it?

Level 2. Putting Christ & Others First

Do Christ and others take priority in your thinking?

Level 3. Personal Freedom from Past, Pain, and Pleasure

Have you faced up to your issues ("your stuff") and put the past in the past?

STAGE TWO – INDEPENDENCE

Level 4. Personal Clarity & Consistency

Are you independently consistent in the Word and Fellowship w/ God? Do you manage your life (time) and resources (money) based on Christ's mission?

Level 5. Working Together with Wisdom

Are you intellectually and emotionally mature enough to do championship teamwork?

Level 6. Kingdom Prayer

Does purposeful prayer fully undergird your life?

STAGE THREE - FRUITION

Level 7. At-ONE-Ment

You are full of the grace of the Holy Spirit and fully available for Christ to live and work through you.

step five

WORKING TOGETHER WITH WISDOM

stage two: independence

reflect

>> WELCOME EVERYONE TO THE SESSION.
>> LET EACH PERSON SHARE FROM THE FOLLOWING QUESTION:

What did the Holy Spirit say or do in your life this past week that helped your personal clarity and consistency?

>> REVIEW HOMEWORK.

How do we grow in understanding according to John 12:16?

How do you react when you fail God in important things? How should you react, with John 13:38 in mind?

Jesus is "the way, the truth, and the life." How can the life of Jesus help you understand God's Word better?

Based on John 14:23-26, how do you develop clarity and consistency in your walk with Christ?

learn

>>READ TOGETHER AND FILL IN THE BLANKS.
>>LEARN ABOUT HIGHER PURPOSE, SHARED VALUES, TOLERANCE, FRIENDSHIP, AND FAITHFUL PRESENCE

THE POWER OF WORKING TOGETHER

Principle #1: Working together requires a sense of higher purpose

> *1 As a prisoner for the Lord, then, I urge you to live a life worthy of the calling you have received. 2 Be completely humble and gentle; be patient, bearing with one another in love. 3 Make every effort to keep the unity of the Spirit through the bond of peace.—Ephesians 4:1-3*

Worthy of the Call (v.1). Paul mentions being a P__________ as a demonstration of the cost he was paying for the Gospel. He did this to set a standard and to lay the groundwork for a team spirit. If he could willingly and voluntarily humble himself and even suffer for the cause, others should do likewise.

Completely Humble (v.2). By "humble," Paul refers to more than an attitude. It involves putting others first and submitting yourself to a higher purpose. In a word—T__________.

Patient (v.2). In teamwork, we should be P_________ when people truly try to live for the cause—even if they fail.

Make Every Effort (v.3). Teamwork *is* W__________. It does not happen naturally but requires maturity and intentionality.

Unity does not mean uniformity. It means working together with wisdom to accomplish singular goals.

What are some good examples of teamwork that you have seen?

 Answers: prisoner, teamwork, patient, work

*"In essentials, **unity**. In nonessentials, **liberty**. In all things, **love**."—Anonymous Quote from Reformation*

Principle #2: Working together requires shared values

"Now I beseech you, brethren, by the name of our Lord Jesus Christ, that ye all speak the same thing, and that there be no divisions among you; but that ye be perfectly joined together in the same mind and in the same judgment."—1 Corinthian 1:10

Same Speech. Mature disciples know how to value one another and disagree A__________. They do not form factions in the Church but seek unity based on a shared commitment to Christ. Same speech is not about uniformity. It is about valuing unity in Christ above all else.

No Divisions. True Christ-followers will tolerate no divisions based on race, nationality, gender, or social status. We must seek the glory of God's K__________ and not our local church, denomination, or religious group.

Same Judgment. Disciples must affirm the Bible as the ultimate guide for Christian behavior and practice. Wise J__________ comes from devotion to God's Word.

DIVERSITY IN THE FAITH

There are nearly 10,000 Christians denominations around the world grouped into 300 major Christian traditions. While some consider this vast diversity in the church a problem, it also represents the unique and beautiful way the gospel reaches people where they are and works to transform them. You do not have to speak a particular language, wear certain kind of clothes, or be born within a specific nation to be a Christian. Christians look like all the peoples of the world. There is a lot of diversity in the Church. God planned it this way.

Answers: agreeably, kingdom, judgment

TOLERANCE

Principle #3: Working together requires patience with others

May the God who gives endurance and encouragement give you the same attitude of mind toward each other that Christ Jesus had.—Romans 15:5

Endurance. Endurance is P__________. Tolerance is a spiritual discipline built on patience. Discipleship involves working through what you understand about God and growing in your knowledge of Jesus Christ. It is an intellectual and E__________ journey. Your growth requires patience, and you should be patient with others in their process of growth.

Encouragement. Our goal when in disagreement with others is ultimately to E__________ the other person. It is never okay to belittle or demean others for what they believe. The Bible says:

Accept the one whose faith is weak, without quarreling over disputable matters. One person's faith allows them to eat anything, but another, whose faith is weak, eats only vegetables. The one who eats everything must not treat with contempt the one who does not, and the one who does not eat everything must not judge the one who does, for God has accepted them. Who are you to judge someone else's servant? To their own master, servants stand or fall. And they will stand, for the Lord is able to make them stand.—
Romans 14:1-4

What are some good examples of tolerance that you have seen?

 Answers: patience, emotional, encourage

THE FRUIT OF THE SPIRIT

The goal of the life of a disciple of Christ is to bear the fruit of the Spirit abundantly. The Bible says:

[22]But the fruit of the Spirit is love, joy, peace, forbearance, kindness, goodness, faithfulness, [23]gentleness and self-control. Against such things there is no law.— Galatians 5:22-23

One role of fellowship and teamwork is to cultivate the fruit of the Spirit in one another.

The Fruit and Teamwork. Notice that all the fruit of the Spirit relates to how we are to live and work together. Even personal principles like joy, peace, and self-control are important in Christian F___________. We have joy together and peace with one another. Essential to the process of teamwork are the traits of self-discipline and self-motivation.

The Fruit and the Gifts. It is also important to make mention of the gifts of the Spirit. The fruit of the Spirit and the spiritual gifts are many times confused. The fruit of the Spirit are C___________traits that represent the character and life of Christ. They are the true evidence of the Spirit of Christ in your life. The spiritual gifts are supernaturally empowered abilities (i.e., teaching, healing) that work to build up the Body of Christ.

The Fruit and Discipleship. The fruit of the Spirit are essential to the process of making D___________. The fruit allow disciples to win the hearts of others, as we demonstrate the compelling nature of Christ's character.

The purpose of the fruit of the Spirit in our lives is to nourish and forest the world.

Answers: fellowship, character, disciples

DEVELOPING FRIENDSHIP

There are many valuable, helpful lessons in the Bible about friendship. There especially is a lot to say about friendship in the Book of Proverbs:

*Whoever would foster love covers over an offense, but whoever repeats the matter separates close **friend**s.—Proverbs 7:9*

*The righteous choose their **friend**s carefully, but the way of the wicked leads them astray.—Proverbs 12:26*

*A **friend** loves at all times, and a brother is born for a time of adversity—Proverbs 17:17*

One who has unreliable friends soon comes to ruin, but there is a friend who sticks closer than a brother.—Proverbs 18:24

*Do not make **friend**s with a hot-tempered person, do not associate with one easily angered.—Proverbs 22:24*

*Wounds from a **friend** can be trusted, but an enemy multiplies kisses.—Proverbs 27:6*

*Do not forsake your **friend** or a **friend** of your family, and do not go to your relative's house when disaster strikes you—better a neighbor nearby than a relative far away.—Proverbs 27:10*

The verses above show that you make and keep friendships through a self-confident display of grace, honesty, and sincere concern. They show the importance of friendliness, while they also share wisdom about making the right personal friendships. Making and developing meaningful friendships is a part of the spiritual growth process.

A church's strength is based on the strength of its friendships. Your ability to make good friends is vital.

FAITHFUL PRESENCE

The idea of Christian community is grounded in the Biblical principle of justice for the poor, weak, and the "least of these." It is driven by hospitality, welcoming the stranger. An authentic Christian culture loves the unlovely and shows compassion to the violent. It draws circles instead of lines. The Christian way is a way of hard-headed, heart-changing love.

Faith and Justice

The prophetic strands of the Old Testament prophet Micah ring true for the Christian disciple:

He has shown you, O mortal, what is good. And what does the Lord require of you? To act justly and to love mercy and to walk humbly with your God.—Micah 6:8

This commitment to justice and mercy flows from the righteousness of God itself. God's righteousness defines justice—it explains what it truly is. Beyond fairness, reciprocity, and even equity—God is concerned about fruitfulness and the elegance of purpose. For God, justice is making things belong and making them useful in the expansion of God's beauty and glory. Justice is not the classic "getting what you are due." It is freely receiving God's grace and freely giving it to others.

Growing in your ability to work together with wisdom means you embrace this purpose. Christian disciples share life together with a commitment to give and receive grace to one another and a heart to share grace with non-Christian neighbors in the world. Read the following report:

> In and around the middle of the second century, there was a series of epidemics that decimated the population.... In those difficult times, there was a sharp contrast between the majority of the population, fleeing the cities and caring only for their own health, and Christians, who took care not only of their own sick but also of many others in the community at large. As a result, there are numerous records of people whose first attraction to Christianity came as they noticed the charitable work of believers, even at the risk of their own lives.*

The most influential Christian witness is the corporate one. Christianity exploded in the early centuries in a non-Christian, even anti-Christian, world because of the faithful presence of the local churches.

*Carlos Cardoza-Orlandi, *To All Nations from All Nations* (Abingdon Press, 2013)

practice: HOSPITALITY

Share with the Lord's people who are in need. Practice hospitality.
—Romans 12:6

Christian unity and teamwork are based on intimacy and a sense of family. The earliest churches met in homes and joined in a weekly meal together. Everyone had something to share, and the strong were led to support the weak. The Church grew phenomenally fast due to the hospitality Christians showed to one another and others. The essential practice for church fellowship, from its beginning until now, is hospitality.

Hospitality is the art of helping everyone feel welcome, no matter what his or her background is, or from wherever he or she comes. There are many different ways to practice hospitality, and there are ways for everyone to get involved.

The following is a list of practices that show hospitality to others:

- **Give away cookies or baked goods**
- **Provide a treat bag for a lonely mother**
- **Prepare dinner for someone**
- **Include someone else's kid on one of your outings**
- **Talk to (and listen to) a widow(-er)**
- **Stay in touch with a bereaved family**
- **Open your home for a Bible Study**
- **Send postcards when traveling**
- **Pick up groceries for an elder or sick person**
- **Mow someone else's lawn**
- **Correspond with a prison inmate**
- **Host a church fellowship event**
- **Send birthday cards or electronic messages**
- **Teach someone something practical, like a resume, sewing, cooking a meal, tying a tie, or changing a tire**

REVIEW THE PRACTICE ON THE NEXT PAGE. REMIND EVERYONE TO **LOOK** FOR THE HOLY SPIRIT IN THEIR DAILY LIVES THROUGHOUT THE WEEK AND TO COMPLETE THE HOMEWORK EXERCISES.

look

>>LOOK FOR THE DECISION-MAKING MOMENTS THROUGHOUT THIS WEEK.
>>REFLECT EACH NIGHT ON HOW WELL YOU NOTICED GOD IN THOSE MOMENTS.

Write down a snapshot of one experience you have this week with working together.

WEEKDAY HOMEWORK

Complete assignment for each day:

day one >> **READ John 15-17 completely. Ask the 5 "W" and the 5 Senses questions.**

who, what, when, where, why?

what can you see, hear, taste, touch, and/or smell?

day two >>	*What are three ways for a disciple to bear fruit according to John 15:1-8?*
day three>>	*Explain the role of Christians in the world according to John 15:26-27?*
day four>>	*What is the role of the Holy Spirit in witnessing based on John 16:8-11?*
day five>>	*In John 17, Jesus prayed for Christian unity. How do you think we can answer that prayer?*

REVIEW OF CHAPTER

This chapter covered the following:

- The impact of working together with wisdom
- Unity in diversity in the body of Christ
- The meaning and importance of tolerance
- Understanding the power of friendship
- The dynamic of faithful presence in the world for mercy and justice

STAGE ONE – DEPENDENCE

Level 1. Seeing Things God's Way
Do you see things God's way? Do you submit to it?

Level 2. Putting Christ & Others First
Do Christ and others take priority in your thinking?

Level 3. Personal Freedom from Past, Pain, and Pleasure
Have you faced up to your issues ("your stuff") and put the past in the past?

STAGE TWO – INDEPENDENCE

Level 4. Personal Clarity & Consistency
Are you independently consistent in the Word and Fellowship w/ God? Do you manage your life (time) and resources (money) based on Christ's mission?

Level 5. Working Together with Wisdom
Are you intellectually and emotionally mature enough to do championship teamwork?

Level 6. Kingdom Prayer
Does purposeful prayer fully undergird your life?

STAGE THREE - FRUITION

Level 7. At-ONE-Ment
You are full of the grace of the Holy Spirit and fully available for Christ to live and work through you.

step six

KINGDOM PRAYER

stage two: independence

reflect

>> WELCOME EVERYONE TO THE SESSION.
>> LET EACH PERSON SHARE FROM THE FOLLOWING QUESTION:

What did the Holy Spirit say or do in your life this past week that helped you work with others with wisdom?

>> REVIEW HOMEWORK.

What are three ways for a disciple to bear fruit according to John 15:1-8?

Explain the role of Christians in the world according to John 15:26-27.

What is the role of the Holy Spirit in witnessing based on John 16:8-11?

How do you think we can answer Jesus' prayer for unity?

learn

>>READ TOGETHER AND FILL IN THE BLANKS.
>>LEARN ABOUT KINGDOM PRAYER AND HOW TO BE EFFECTIVE, PERSISTENT, AND HEARTFELT IN PRAYER.

Kingdom Prayer

Principle #1: Prayer expands God's kingdom

> *9 Our Father in heaven, hallowed be your name, 10 your kingdom come, your will be done, on earth as it is in heaven. 11 Give us today our daily bread. 12 And forgive us our debts, as we also have forgiven our debtors. 13 And lead us not into temptation, but deliver us from the evil one.—Matthew 6:9-13*

Hallowed be Your Name (v.9). Much prayer centers on your personal needs and concerns. Kingdom prayer focuses, first of all, on God's glory.

Your will be done (v.10). Kingdom prayer prays for the E__________ of God's glory and kingdom in the world. God already rules over everything from heaven, but His earthly kingdom is expanded when people are saved and willingly submit to His will.

Our daily bread (v.11). Kingdom prayer is M__________ prayer that understands how to depend on God for everything. As we grow, we learn to lean on God more and more.

Forgive as we forgive (v.12). God's plan is to R__________ people, and not destroy lives. Forgiveness is essential to expanding the kingdom.

Deliver us (v. 13). The image behind this prayer is Israel's exodus from Egypt and wandering in the wilderness. People in Jesus' day saw themselves in a spiritual W__________ experience and in need of deliverance from a new Pharaoh, Satan. Kingdom prayer overcomes the bondage of the devil.

What lessons do you learn from the Lord's Prayer?

 Answers: expansion, mature, renew, wilderness

Kingdom prayer is effective, persistent, heartfelt prayer that expands God's kingdom on earth as it is in the heavens.

WHAT IS EFFECTIVE PRAYER?

Principle #2: Kingdom prayer is effective

> [16]*Come and hear, all you who fear God; let me tell you what he has done for me.* [17]*I cried out to him with my mouth; his praise was on my tongue.* [18]*If I had cherished sin in my heart, the Lord would not have listened;* [9]*but God has surely listened and has heard my prayer.* [20]*Praise be to God, who has not rejected my prayer or withheld his love from me!*—Psalms 66:16-20

Come and hear (v.16). In the Psalm, David is testifying about his prayer life.

Praise (v.17). David's prayer was expressive and very P__________. He began with thanks and praise to God openly.

Repent (v.18). David presented his whole H__________ to God, and he confessed all known sins.

> *"Though you probe my heart, though you examine me at night and test me, you will find that I have planned no evil; my mouth has not transgressed."*—Psalm 17:3

Connect (vv.19-20). David's experience in prayer involved a real C__________ with God.

> *"My heart says of you, "Seek his face!" Your face, Lord, I will seek."*—Psalms 27:8

Effective prayer seeks a real holy connection with a holy God to make a powerful impact.

Answers: passionate, heart, connection

PERSISTENCE IN PRAYER

Principle #3: Kingdom prayer is persistent

[1]Then Jesus told his disciples a parable to show them that they should always pray and not give up. [2]He said: "In a certain town there was a judge who neither feared God nor cared what people thought. [3]And there was a widow in that town who kept coming to him with the plea, 'Grant me justice against my adversary.'"—Luke 18:1-3

Always Pray (v.1). Effective prayer trusts God for all things. It makes decisions based on God's revealed W__________ and action. It puts the outcomes of prayer firmly in God's hands.

They Should Not Give Up (vv.2-3). Effective prayer is effective because it diligently seeks God for an A__________. In the story, the widow "kept coming" until her issue was resolved. This kind of prayer is earnest even when the situation is not desperate. It is confident in its C__________, and this confidence rests in a mature faith (i.e., a faith refined through the levels and stages of faith.)

Persistent prayer involves praying over one's day every day and possessing the habit of praying over situations as they arise throughout the day.

LORD, you are the God who saves me; day and night I cry out to you. May my prayer come before you; turn your ear to my cry.—***Psalm 88:1-2***

 Answers: will, answer, conviction

HEARTFELT PRAYER

Principle #4: Kingdom prayer is heartfelt

> ***Therefore confess your sins to each other and pray for each other so that you may be healed. The [heartfelt] prayer of a righteous person is powerful and effective.—James 5:16***

Effective prayer is earnest, and it is heartfelt. Acknowledging God in the middle of a situation motivates and convicts us. Your emotions are freely and powerfully engaged. This real emotion is often necessary to pray with the earnestness, truthfulness, and consistency needed to press toward an answer.

Here are some ways to engage your heart in prayer:

Pray for clarity. Ask God to show you God's own H__________ in the situation.

Read Psalms. Read Psalms that relate to the situation you are experiencing. Usually, you will be able to find one through a quick reading through the Book of Psalms.)

Prayer with others. C__________ with others in prayer about the situation. Often, hearing someone else's heart stirs your own.

Confess Victory. Claim J__________ in the situation. See sickness and the oppression of Satan as injustice and seek for wrongs to be made right.

The most powerful form of prayer is the heart reaching out in love to God.

Do you ever struggle with persistent prayer?

Is your regular prayer life lively and heartfelt?

Answers: heart, Connect, justice

HOW THE SPIRIT HELPS

The Holy Spirit is our Senior Partner. There are several ways the Holy Spirit guides you and aids you in Kingdom Prayer. Note four ways outlined as confirmation, clarity, character, and calling.

Confirmation. He provides an I__________ W__________. This very personal witness a strong inward conviction that we belong to God, accompanied by peace, joy, and a sense of God's love. It also involves a desire to do what is right in your life.

The Spirit himself testifies with our spirit that we are God's children.—Rom. 8:16

Clarity. He leads us into all T__________ and reminds us of God's Word.

But when he, the Spirit of truth, comes, he will guide you into all the truth. He will not speak on his own; he will speak only what he hears, and he will tell you what is yet to come.—John 16:13

But the Advocate, the Holy Spirit, whom the Father will send in my name, will teach you all things and will remind you of everything I have said to you.—John 14:26

Moral Character. He empowers us to overcome T__________and the flesh.

For if you live according to the flesh, you will die; but if by the Spirit you put to death the misdeeds of the body, you will live.—Rom. 8:13

Calling on God. He assists us in P__________.

In the same way, the Spirit helps us in our weakness. We do not know what we ought to pray for, but the Spirit himself intercedes for us through wordless groans.—Rom. 8:26

 Answers: inner, witness, truth, temptation, prayer

When we learn how to see things God's way, put Christ and others first, find personal freedom, consistency, and clarity, and our place in the bigger picture, our faith is set for our prayers to be unhindered, focused, faithful, and effective.

MOVING TO FRUITION

Independence is a major achievement. Many people get too personal clarity and consistency or even working together with wisdom and stop seeking to grow. There is more.

God intends for us to be fruitful. Jesus says:

> *I am the true vine, and my Father is the gardener. He cuts off every branch in me that bears no fruit, while every branch that does bear fruit he prunes so that it will be even more fruitful.—John 15:1-2*

God not only wants for you to be fruitful, but He wants you to be "even more fruitful." The next step past Kingdom Prayer is finding a spiritual alignment with God. This level of maturity is represented in the word "atonement," which comes from the literal combination of the words "at" and "one."

When we are spiritually "at-one" with God, this spiritual unity brings abundant fruit in our personal lives and, through us, in the lives of others.

practice: P.R.A.Y.

FELLOWSHIP WITH GOD

One of the main words for prayer in the Old Testament is tefillah. This prayer is not merely asking for something. It is more personal fellowship with God, where you come together with God and reflect on your heart and your life. It is a time to examine one's life in the light of the beauty of God's holiness and to focus your heart on God.

This prayer precedes other forms of prayer and is the foundation for effective prayer. You can use acronym the P-R-A-Y below as a guide for effective "tefillah" prayer.

The P.R.A.Y. Method

P	Praise Count your blessings and recall how God provided each one. Thank God for each one and praise God for how God did what God did. (Read Psalm 103:2)
R	Reflect Read the Bible and use God's Word to reflect on your heart and your life. Repent of any sins that come to mind. (Read Heb. 4:12)
A	Adore Ask God to connect with your mind and heart. Ask the Holy Spirit to pour out God's love into your heart in a real and meaningful way. (Read Rom. 5:5)
Y	Yield Lift every issue you are facing—good and bad—to God. Surrender every worry and concern. (Read Ps. 46:10)

REVIEW THE PRACTICE ABOVE. REMIND EVERYONE TO **LOOK** FOR THE HOLY SPIRIT IN THEIR DAILY LIVES THROUGHOUT THE WEEK AND TO COMPLETE THE HOMEWORK EXERCISES.

look

>>LOOK FOR THE DECISION-MAKING MOMENTS THROUGHOUT THIS WEEK.
>>REFLECT EACH NIGHT ON HOW WELL YOU NOTICED GOD IN THOSE MOMENTS.

Write down a snapshot of one experience you have this week with corporate prayer.

WEEKDAY HOMEWORK

Complete assignment for each day:

day one >> READ John 18-21 completely. Ask the 5 "W" and the 5 Senses questions.

who, what, when, where, why?

what can you see, hear, taste, touch, and/or smell?

day two >> *John 18 begins with Jesus in the Garden of Gethsemane. How does John's account relate to Matthew 26:47-56?*

day three>> *How do you think Jesus' prayer and preparation in Gethsemane prepared him for his trial and crucifixion?*

day four>> *On a separate page, outline and describe the actual death of Jesus as recorded in John 19:28-37 in your own words.*

day five>> *What do you think John 20:19-23 is teaching?*

BONUS QUESTION>> What might the reference to the 153 fish mean?

REVIEW OF CHAPTER

This chapter covered the following:

- We can have freedom from our past, our pain, and our personal temptations
- Our path to freedom involves being like Christ and allowing Christ to renew us
- We must see things God's way and put Christ and others first before we can experience true freedom
- Renewal involves being washed from sin, woundedness, and wicked thoughts

STAGE ONE – DEPENDENCE

Level 1. Seeing Things God's Way
Do you see things God's way? Do you submit to it?

Level 2. Putting Christ & Others First
Do Christ and others take priority in your thinking?

Level 3. Personal Freedom from Past, Pain, and Pleasure
Have you faced up to your issues ("your stuff") and put the past in the past?

STAGE TWO – INDEPENDENCE

Level 4. Personal Clarity & Consistency
Are you independently consistent in the Word and Fellowship w/ God? Do you manage your life (time) and resources (money) based on Christ's mission?

Level 5. Working Together with Wisdom
Are you intellectually and emotionally mature enough to do championship teamwork?

Level 6. Kingdom Prayer
Does purposeful prayer fully undergird your life?

STAGE THREE - FRUITION

Level 7. At-ONE-Ment
You are full of the grace of the Holy Spirit and fully available for Christ to live and work through you.

step seven

AT-ONE-MENT

stage three: fruition

reflect

>> WELCOME EVERYONE TO THE SESSION.
>> LET EACH PERSON SHARE FROM THE FOLLOWING QUESTION:

What did the Holy Spirit say or do in your life this past week that helped you practice Kingdom Prayer?

>> REVIEW HOMEWORK.

How does John's account of Jesus in the Garden of Gethsemane compare to Matthew's account?

How did Kingdom Prayer prepare Jesus for his trial and crucifixion?

What part of the record of Jesus' death spoke to you when you made your outline?

What do you think John 20:19-23 is teaching?

Bonus Question: What do you think the 153 fish represent?

learn

>>READ TOGETHER AND FILL IN THE BLANKS.
>>LEARN ABOUT UNION, BEING FRUITFUL, AND HOW TO MAKE DISCIPLES.

AT-ONE-MENT

Principle #1: Union with God is the goal of maturity

[22] I have given them the glory that you gave me, that they may be one as we are one—[23] I in them and you in me—so that they may be brought to complete unity. Then the world will know that you sent me and have loved them even as you have loved me.—John 17:22-23

Glory (v.22). God's glory was his M__________ P__________. In the Old Testament, it resided in the Most Holy Place in the Temple in Jerusalem, but it eventually left God's people after centuries of sin. In Jesus, the glory returned, and when Jesus returned to heaven, the glory would rest with the Church. Here are some verses about God's glory resting with his people:

When Solomon finished praying, fire came down from heaven and consumed the burnt offering and the sacrifices, and the glory of the Lord filled the temple.—2 Chronicles 7:1

[34] Then the cloud covered the tent of meeting, and the glory of the Lord filled the tabernacle. [35] Moses could not enter the tent of meeting because the cloud had settled on it, and the glory of the Lord filled the tabernacle. —Exodus 40:34-35

The Word became flesh and made his dwelling among us. We have seen his glory, the glory of the one and only Son, who came from the Father, full of grace and truth.—John 1:14

They May Be One (v.22-23). Jesus prayed that the Church would be united in the E__________ of God in Jesus Christ. God powerfully showed up in Jesus' earthly life and ministry. Jesus shows up in his disciples who walk in unity with him.

Describe a time you felt especially close to God.

 Answers: manifest, presence, experience

What Does Atonement Mean?

Atonement is a compound word that means to be "at-one." It comes from the idea that God wants to be "at-one" with His people and wants His people to be "at-one" with Him. Early in God's story, it showed God visiting Adam and Eve in the Garden in the cool of the day. (Genesis 3:8) God had always desired to be close to us.

THE OLD TESTAMENT ATONEMENT

In the story of God's people, God had Moses build a Tent for God's presence to abide with His people. This Tent was placed at the center of their encampment—when Israel wandered in the wilderness—and at the center of the nation when Israel lived in the Promised Land. God's glory—His manifest presence—was meant to unify God's people and to give them life.

Once each year, God's people would gather together and think over the year they just had. They would reflect on their relationship with God and with one another, mainly how they fell short. All of their prayers and confessions together would lead up to the Day of Atonement when the High Priest would go before the glory of God in the Most Holy Place for their sins against God and one another to be forgiveness and purged. In this way, their hearts were to be unburdened and turned back to loving God and others. Everything separating them from God and one another was erased, and they were made, in fact, "at-one."

THE NEW ATONEMENT

Regular offerings were made throughout the year to maintain the atonement. All these sacrifices were meant to turn the heart back to God. However, the sacrifice of Jesus has the effect of transforming the heart. The Bible says:

> *The blood of goats and bulls and the ashes of a heifer sprinkled on those who are ceremonially unclean sanctify them so that they are outwardly clean. How much more, then, will the blood of Christ, who through the eternal Spirit offered himself unblemished to God, cleanse our consciences from acts that lead to death, so that we may serve the living God!—Hebrews 9:13-14*

Spiritual maturity is defined by this transformation of our hearts and minds, and it is shown to be real by our fruitfulness in Christ.

HOW DO WE BEAR FRUIT?

Principle #2: We bear fruit by God's Word and Spirit

[5] "I am the vine; you are the branches. If you remain in me and I in you, you will bear much fruit; apart from me you can do nothing. [6] If you do not remain in me, you are like a branch that is thrown away and withers; such branches are picked up, thrown into the fire and burned. [7] If you remain in me and my words remain in you, ask whatever you wish, and it will be done for you. [8] This is to my Father's glory, that you bear much fruit, showing yourselves to be my disciples. —John 15:5-7

Much Fruit (v. 5). Disciples produce D____________. The ultimate fruit disciples bear are more disciples. The fruit also signifies the fruit of the Spirit, which are the character traits of Christ. The two ideas are connected. When we abundantly produce the fruit of the Spirit, we naturally produce more disciples of Christ.

Remain In Me (v.6). Jesus challenges his disciples to stay connected with him and warns that disconnection results in unfruitfulness. You cannot produce a disciple of Christ without Christ's P___________.

My Words (v.7). Remaining in Christ is the experience of walking in the Holy Spirit and the power of A___________ prayer. Jesus shows that this is possible for a disciple only when you study and keep the teachings of Christ.

My Father's Glory (v.8). We glorify God when we display the C___________ of Christ and develop new disciples. God is honored with the multiplying of disciples. (cf. Prov. 14:28)

We bear the fruit of character, good works, and new disciples as we walk in union with Christ. We do this by following God's Word, giving ourselves to Kingdom Prayer, and actively seeking to glorify God every day.

 Answers: disciples, power, answered, character

WHAT'S NEXT?

Growing to maturity in Christ is just the beginning. Christians never stop growing.

Principle #3: Growth continues in our giftings and calling

[Christ] is the one we proclaim, admonishing and teaching everyone with all wisdom, so that we may present everyone fully mature in Christ.—Colossians 1:28

Proclaiming Spiritual Gifts. Just like every person is born with a set of T__________, every Christian is provided a set of spiritual gifts. A spiritual gift is a divinely inspired or empowered ability that the Christian can use at will.

[7]Now to each one the manifestation of the Spirit is given for the common good. [8]To one there is given through the Spirit a message of wisdom, to another a message of knowledge by means of the same Spirit, [9]to another faith by the same Spirit, to another gifts of healing by that one Spirit, [10]to another miraculous powers, to another prophecy, to another distinguishing between spirits, to another speaking in different kinds of tongues, and to still another the interpretation of tongues. [11]All these are the work of one and the same Spirit, and he distributes them to each one, just as he determines.—1 Corinthians 12:7-1

[6]For this reason I remind you to fan into flame the gift of God, which is in you through the laying on of my hands.—2 Timothy 1:6

Admonishing for Vocation. Your combination of natural talents and spiritual gifts empower you for your V__________. A spiritual vocation is different from a secular career. Your career is what you do in the world to make money. Your vocation is the job you have in God's kingdom.

*[28]And God has placed in the church first of all apostles, second prophets, third teachers, then miracles, then gifts of healing, of helping, of guidance, and of different kinds of tongues.—*1 Corinthians 12:28

Teaching for Calling. Sometimes the word "calling" is used the same way as "vocation." However, a calling is different. Your calling is your specific A__________ at a particular time and place.

Answers: talents, vocation, assignment

MAKING DISCIPLES

The disciple-making process is a team effort. It involves four levels of teaching and training.

Principle #3: Disciplemaking is a Team Process

You then, my son, be strong in the grace that is in Christ Jesus. And the things you have heard me say in the presence of many witnesses entrust to reliable people who will also be qualified to teach others.— 2 Timothy 2:1-2

Level 1—Leader. ("Things you heard *me* say.") Paul approached Timothy from the position of the Leader of the ministry. Paul provided Timothy in-depth training and encouraged him to follow Paul's example.

The Leader's role is to train the trainers and assign them to their work. The in-depth training Paul provided as a leader is the subject of his two letters to Timothy. It included instructions on what Timothy's role was, what he was to teach, how to P__________, how to behave, tips on how to relate to people, and how to deal with conflict.

Level 2—Coach. ("*You* then be strong.") Timothy served as the discipleship ministry C__________. His role was to take what he had learned and to train others to be effective at instructing new believers and unbelievers about Christ's teachings.

The coach selects participants who show a desire to be discipled and who will be committed to the DSG process. The coach leads people through the Spiritual Maturity Workbook and the Disciplemakers Booklet, adding helpful tips and encouragement to the participants.

Level 3—Disciple. ("Reliable people who are qualified") Timothy was to choose disciples to be trained to be disciplemakers. They were selected so they could instruct new believers and unbelievers about the life and teachings of Jesus Christ. (Leaders and Coaches must do this work as well.) A selected disciple had to meet two qualifications: this person had to be 1) R__________ and 2) T__________.

 Answers: prepare, coach, reliable, teachable

The role of the disciple is to witness to others (see Practice for the "WITNESS" Model) and encourage beginners in the faith to seek after spiritual maturity. Using this model, disciples share God's S__________ from the Bible and their own personal stories with God to help others see God working in their lives.

Level 4—Beginner (the "others as well") A beginner is a long-time or new B__________ who is being led to a fresh commitment to discipleship. This person is learning the basics of the faith, such as how to turn from sin and trust God for a new life, how to be a part of the Church and understand how it works, and what God's ultimate plan is all about.

Beginners start with a recognition of God's divine presence in their lives and must be nurtured to explore their faith through Christian E__________, godly counsel, and prayer.

MOVING FORWARD

When you walk in spiritual union with God, you are fruitful in your character, good works, and ultimately in making new disciples. As you move forward from this level of maturity, you are fully empowered to make disciples and expand God's kingdom with supernatural success.

Remember, it takes time to walk through the Spiritual Maturity Pathway. God will teach you the lessons of stages and steps many times before it becomes a solid part of your character. Do not confuse learning a what a principle is and learning to apply the principle regularly. The one step leads to the other, but they are not the same.

Now that you have completed Series 4 using the Spiritual Maturity Workbook, you should spend some time in one-on-one training with your coach. This time will focus on you reflect on where you are in this Pathway and how the Holy Spirit is leading you to grow. It also should be a time when you challenge yourself to read through the Bible. (You may also consider reading along with an audio Bible version.)

Series 5 involves specific training on disciplemaking. You will see the full picture of God's plan to transform the world and learn how to effectively reach and teach people in the power of the Holy Spirit. The Practice and homework following this page, however, will get you start on this path even now.

Answers: story, believer, example

practice: WITNESS

W	**Wisdom from the Word – Deut. 4:6** *Godly wisdom can help everyone. Share wisdom and inspiration from your daily devotions, Bible Study, or weekly sermons.*
I	**Inspiration – Phil. 2:1-2** *Always seek to add value to people through your words and actions. Encourage people with an upbeat, positive attitude.*
T	**Testimony – 1 John 1:1** *Share your personal testimony of God's blessings in your life. Be excited about God's work in your life.*
N	**Name of Jesus—Acts 4:12** *Always give glory to the Name of Jesus in your day to day living. When sharing your faith, do not fail to mention the only Name that saves.*
E	**Example – 1 Tim. 4:12** *Be a humble example of a godly life. Be careful not to often put yourself in compromising positions where your good intentions can easily be taken as bad actions.*
S	**Salvation – Gal. 6:1** *Know and share God's plan of salvation that we are saved by grace through faith, and renewed to live a godly life.*
S	**Spirit of God – 1 Cor. 2:4-5** *Pray daily to follow the leading of the Spirit and for His empowerment as you witness for Christ.*

THIS IS THE LAST SESSION. REVIEW THE **PRACTICE** ABOVE AND THE **HOMEWORK** EXERCISE..ENCOURAGE THE GROUP TO REMEMBER THE SEVENS STEPS AND EVALUATE THEIR GROWTH.

HOMEWORK

WRITE YOUR PERSONAL TESTIMONY

*They triumphed over [Satan] by the blood of the Lamb and by the word of **their testimony** ...Revelation 12:11*

Write down your testimony. Pray for insight on what God would like you to share. You may not feel your testimony is very exciting, but be encouraged that it is exciting to become a Christian, no matter how it happened. You can start by finishing the following opening sentences:

Before I trusted Christ I ....

What was the key problem, emotion, situation or attitude you were dealing with? What motivated you? What were your actions? How did you try to satisfy your inner needs?

When I trusted Christ he ...

What did Christ do to change you? What was happening at the time? What people or problems influenced your decision?

After I trusted Christ I ...

How has your life in Christ made a difference? How has his forgiveness impacted you? How have your thoughts, attitudes and emotions changed?

REVIEW OF CHAPTER

This chapter covered the following:

- The meaning and importance of atonement
- How to bear spiritual fruit
- What comes after the steps and stages of maturity
- How to share your faith using the WITNESS Method

STAGE ONE – DEPENDENCE

Level 1. Seeing Things God's Way

Do you see things God's way? Do you submit to it?

Level 2. Putting Christ & Others First

Do Christ and others take priority in your thinking?

Level 3. Personal Freedom from Past, Pain, and Pleasure

Have you faced up to your issues ("your stuff") and put the past in the past?

STAGE TWO – INDEPENDENCE

Level 4. Personal Clarity & Consistency

Are you independently consistent in the Word and Fellowship w/ God? Do you manage your life (time) and resources (money) based on Christ's mission?

Level 5. Working Together with Wisdom

Are you intellectually and emotionally mature enough to do championship teamwork?

Level 6. Kingdom Prayer

Does purposeful prayer fully undergird your life?

STAGE THREE - FRUITION

Level 7. At-ONE-Ment

You are full of the grace of the Holy Spirit and fully available for Christ to live and work through you.

APPENDIX

THE TABERNACLE MODEL

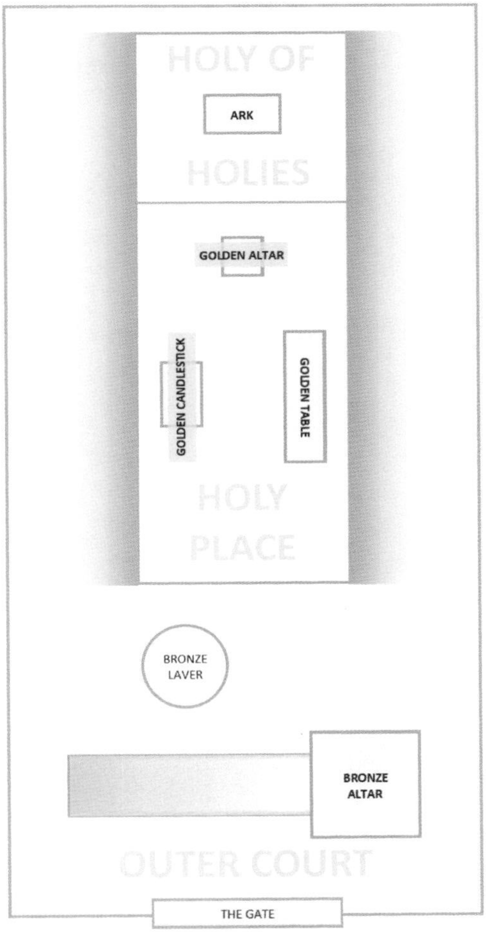

DIAGRAM OF THE TABERNACLE
Not to Scale

The discipleship process included in this workbook comes out of a study on the Tabernacle of Moses. The Tabernacle was central to the life of God's people, both for worship and as a teaching tool to understand the ways of God. The Tabernacle was patterned after a heavenly model, and its structure and the worship held there had symbolic spiritual significance.

Hebrews 8:5 says, "They serve at a sanctuary that is a copy and shadow of what is in heaven. This is why Moses was warned when he was about to build the tabernacle: 'See to it that you make everything according to the pattern shown you on the mountain.'"

The diagram above shows the basic structure of the Tabernacle of Moses. It involves three major areas and seven stations. The three areas are as follows: 1) the outer court (courtyard), 2) Holy Place, and 3) the Holy of Holies.

The seven stations are: 1) The Entry Gate; 2) The Bronze Altar; 3) the Bronze Laver; 4) the Golden Lampstand, 5) the Golden Table of Showbread, 6) the Golden Altar; and 7) the Ark of the Covenant. The outline below shows how each area and station relates to a process of maturity for the believer in Christ.

OUTER COURT/STAGE OF DEPENDENCE	
In the Tabernacle, worshippers brought their sacrifices, but were ***dependent*** *on priests to carry out the work.*	
The Entry Gate Seeing Things God's Way	*The experience of entering the Temple was like moving out of the world into a embassy of heaven. The effect was a paradigm shift as the worshipper is a reminder of the centrality of God.*
The Bronze Altar Putting Christ and Others First	*The Bronze Altar received the sacrifices from the people. In Christ, we are told to be a living sacrifice, giving our bodies in service to Christ and others. (Rom. 12)*
The Laver Personal Freedom from Past, Pain, and Pleasure	*A priest only functioned as a priest as they wore the priestly garments. When they entered the Tabernacle for service, they would remove their old clothes and wash their hands and feet in the laver before putting on their priestly robes and role. This is what Paul had in mind when writing Ephesians 4:20-24.*
HOLY PLACE/STAGE OF INDEPENDENCE	
Only priest who had been trained in holiness were allowed into the Holy Place.	
The Lampstand Clarity and Consistency	*The first station for a priest in the sanctuary was the Lampstand. The Lampstand provided the only light for the room and was to be trimmed morning and evening. This represents the principle of illumination.*
The Golden Table Working Together with Wisdom	*On the Table of Showbread—as called the Table of the Presence—twelve loaves of fresh bread sprinkled with frankincense were placed. Each loaf represented a tribe of Israel and all the loaves together represented the unity of God's people in the Presence of God.*
Golden Altar Effective Prayer	*Twice daily, a priest would offer incense and a prayer of self-reflection on behalf of God's people on the short altar of incense in the Sanctuary. The smoke represented the prayers of God's people, and the fragrance that filled the room represented the holy Presence of God.*
HOLY OF HOLIES/ATONEMENT	
The whole purpose of the Tabernacle was to maintain union between God and His people.	
Holy of Holies At-ONE-Ment/ Fruition	*The Holy of Holies is where the Shekinah (manifested) Glory of God rested on the Mercy Seat atop the Ark of the Covenant. Access was restricted to only the High Priest, who could enter once a year. At that time, he made a sacrifice of atonement for the forgiveness of sins and to revive the relationship between God and God's people. This resulted in the abundant fruitfulness of God's people.*

98769917R00062

Made in the USA
Columbia, SC
06 July 2018